Who Says a Dog Goes Bow-wow?

A Doubleday Book for Young Readers

Who Says

By Hank De Zutter
Illustrated by Suse MacDonald

a Dog Goes Bow-wow?

A Doubleday Book for Young Readers
Published by
Delacorte Press
Bantam Doubleday Dell Publishing Group, Inc.
666 Fifth Avenue
New York, New York 10103
Doubleday and the portrayal of
an anchor with a dolphin are trademarks of
Bantam Doubleday Dell Publishing Group, Inc.

Text copyright © 1993 by Hank De Zutter
Illustrations copyright © 1993 by Suse MacDonald

Library of Congress Cataloging in Publication Data

De Zutter, Hank.
Who says a dog goes bow-wow? / Hank De Zutter ;
illustrated by Suse MacDonald.
    p.   cm.
Summary: Presents animal sounds in many
different languages.
ISBN: 0-385-30659-8
1. Onomatopoeia—Juvenile literature.
2. Animal sounds—Juvenile literature.
[1. Animal sounds.]   I. MacDonald, Suse, ill.
II. Title.
P119.D4   1993
418—dc20   92-4232   CIP   AC

PRINTED IN ITALY

February 1993

10 9 8 7 6 5 4 3 2 1

I would like to acknowledge the assistance of
the students and faculty of LaSalle Language
Academy, a very special Chicago public school.
I am especially grateful to fifth-grade teacher
Regina McClellan, the class of 1993, and the
following bilinguists who helped me gather and
check the animal sounds as rendered into the
various languages:
Barbara Berndt · Sjaak Blaauw · Lisbeth
Christensen · Anna Czerwinski · Barbara Jurasek ·
Hediye Kot · Monica Lima · Maria Litsas ·
Madeleine Mirani · Birgit Olk · Rainer Porthan ·
Gopaa Prachand · Chiharu Sato · Insawn Saw ·
Peter Soljak · Marwin Tanattanawin

I would also like to thank the following people
for their help in gathering and checking
animal sounds:
Omiros Avramides · Beatrice Canetti · Anna
Droumeva · Arpád Haragos · Mira Jovicic ·
Nurcihan Kesim · Simona Kessler · Menno Kohn ·
So Jin Kwak · Birgit Moosmüller · Tachi
Nagasawa · Karin Petríková · Ilana Pikarsky · Gerd
J. Plessl · Irina Reylander · Maria Strarz-Kánska ·
Ulf Toregard · Jian-mei Wang · Montse F. Yañez

This book is not the final authority on international
animal sounds; it merely offers some of the more
prevalent possibilities. The spellings are phonetic
renderings of the sounds designed for readers
of American English. Each sound is merely one of
often several choices available in each language;
English speakers themselves can choose arf or
woof for a dog, or chirp or tweet for a bird.

The full-color collages were created by cutting
shapes from hand-colored tissue paper and
applying them to a rag board using a mixture of
metylan cellulose and jade PVA adhesive.
The text of this book is set in 36 point Helvetica,
14 point Bookman Medium, and 12 point Bookman
Light Italic. Typography is by Lynn Braswell.

*To my daughter, Amanda,
her classmates at LaSalle
Language Academy, and
all other children who dare to
ask questions in any language*
H.DZ.

*My thanks to Eric Carle,
who shared his technique*
S.M.

Who says a dog goes "bow-wow"?
Not the dog.
And who says a pig goes "oink-oink"?
Not the hog.

In Britain, for instance, or the U.S. of A.,
A dog barks "bow-wow," or so people say.

But the same dog in Germany, Greece, or Japan
Barks with a "woo-woo," "gav-gav," or "wan-wan."

Where people live and what language *they're* using
Determine what animals say to us humans.

So read now with us (bark with us too)
As we learn the sounds of an international zoo.

How does a dog bark?

How-how · *Finnish, Turkish, Russian, Polish*
Huf-huf · *Hebrew, Farsi*
Vow-vow · *Danish*
Ow-ow · *Lithuanian*
Wan-wan · *Japanese*
Wah-wah · *French*
Woof-woof · *Dutch*
Bow-bow · *Italian*
Ar-ar · *Serbo-Croatian*
Hong-hong · *Thai*
Mong-mong · *Korean*
Wang-wang · *Chinese*
Bow-wow · *English*

How does a mouse speak?

Squeak-squeak · *English*
Cleek-cleek · *Hebrew*
Cweek-cweek · *Greek*
Cheek-cheek · *Polish*
Cui-cui · *Spanish*
Peep-peep · *Russian*
Peev-peev · *Danish*
Chee-chee · *Lithuanian*
Seet-seet · *Indonesian*
I-i-i-i · *German, Finnish*
Ead-ead · *Thai*
Chu-chu · *Japanese*
Chee-chee · *Chinese*

How does a pig grunt?

Oink-oink · *English, German*
Ot-ot · *Vietnamese*
Euf-euf · *Danish*
Nof-nof · *Swedish*
Ciuk-ciuk · *Lithuanian*
Grok-grok · *Indonesian*
Roh-roh · *Finnish*
Gwa-gwa · *French*
Hru-hru · *Russian*
Buu-buu · *Japanese*
Ggooll-ggooll · *Korean*
Hu-lu · *Chinese*
Kweek-kweek · *Polish*
Knorr-knorr · *Dutch*

Gobble-gobble · *English*
Gloo-gloo · *French, Greek*
Goo-goo · *Chinese*
Goul-goul · *Polish*
Ga-ga · *Serbo-Croatian*
Gok-gok · *Thai*
Klok-klok · *Dutch*
Kluk-kluk · *Indonesian*
Ader-ader · *Hebrew*
Buldu-buldu · *Lithuanian*

What does a turkey say?

Cock-a-doodle-doo · *English*
Coco-rico · *French*
Ku-ku-ree-ku · *Polish*
Ku-ke-le-koo · *Dutch*
Kee-klee-ky · *Danish*
Kee-kee-ree-kee · *Spanish, Italian*
Ka-ka-ree-ku · *Lithuanian*
Ku-ku-ru-ku · *Turkish*
Ku-ku-ru-yuk · *Indonesian*
Kucko-kieku · *Finnish*
Ghoo-ghoolie-ghoo · *Farsi*
Kokke-kokko · *Japanese*
Wo-wo-wo · *Chinese*
Guggeru-guuhh · *Swiss German*
Ko-kee-o · *Korean*
Ek-ee-ek-egg · *Thai*

How does a rooster crow?

How does a cow sound?

Moo · *English, Indonesian, Lithuanian,
Danish, Italian, Swedish,
German, Polish, Greek*
Maw-maw · *Thai*
Meuh-meuh · *French*
Boeh-boeh · *Dutch*
E-bah · *Ethiopian*
Um-moo · *Korean*
Ah-moo · *Finnish*

What does a lamb say?

B-a-a-a-a · *English, Danish, Swedish*
M-a-a-a-a · *German, Finnish*
M-i-e-h · *Chinese*
M-a-a-a-ay · *Japanese, Farsi, Dutch*
B-a-ay · *Polish, French*
Em-beck · *Indonesian*

Yaong-yaong · *Korean*
Me-yong · *Indonesian*
Nyan-nyan · *Japanese*
Meow · *English, Chinese, Farsi,*
Lithuanian, French, Polish, Thai,
Danish, Dutch, German, Turkish,
Italian, Finnish, Swedish

How does a cat sound?

How does a monkey chatter?

Keek-keek · *Indonesian, Japanese*
Chee-chee · *English*
Jiak-jiak · *Thai*
Szeek-szeek · *Polish*
Hoo-hoo · *Dutch*
Twee-twee · *Swedish*

How does a crow cry?

Caw-caw · *English*
Kva-kva · *Lithuanian*
Kroak-kroak · *French*
Kaa-kaa · *Japanese*
Kuck-kuck · *Indonesian*
Gua-gua · *Chinese*
Ggakk-ggakk · *Korean*
Ga-ga · *Thai, Serbo-Croatian*
Kra-kra · *Polish, Dutch, Swedish, Finnish, Greek*

How does a bee sound?

Bzzz · *English, Dutch, Italian, Greek, French*
Z-z-z-z-z · *Polish, Indonesian*
Boon-boon · *Japanese*
Weng-weng · *Chinese*
Hueng-hueng · *Thai*
Surrrr · *Finnish*
Sorr-orrr · *Swedish*
Dzh-zh · *Russian*

How does a cricket sound?

Chirp-chirp · *English, Lithuanian*
Zhir-zhir · *Finnish, Swedish, Dutch*
Cree-cree · *French, Italian, Greek*
Jeed-jeed · *Thai*
Jee-jee · *Chinese*

How does a chicken talk?

Cluck-cluck · *English*
Tok-tok · *Dutch*
Jeek-jeek · *Farsi*
Ge-ge · *Chinese*
Kot-kot · *French*
Git-git-gidak · *Turkish*
Ga-ga-ga-gak · *German*
Petok-petok · *Indonesian*
Cheep-cheep · *Lithuanian*
Pee-pee · *Serbo-Croatian*
Ku-ku · *Japanese*
Ko-ko-ko · *Polish*
Ka-ka-ka · *Greek*
Klook-klook · *Danish*
Gook-gook · *Thai*

How does a horse whinny?

E-a-ha-ha · *Polish, Finnish, Lithuanian*
Hee-hee-heen · *Japanese*
Hee-ehee-hee · *German*
Nay-ay-ay-ay · *English*
Nee-ee-ee · *Indonesian*
E-go-go · *Russian*
Hee-hee-hee · *Thai*
Heen-eek · *Dutch*
E-e-e-e-e · *Italian*
Hee-eeng · *Korean*
Eee-haw · *Farsi*
See-ee-ee · *Chinese*
V-r-ee-nsk · *Danish*

How does a duck speak?

Quack-quack · *English, Turkish, Dutch, German*
Kwa-kwa · *Polish, Italian*
Krak-krak · *Serbo-Croatian*
Kvaak-kvaak · *Finnish, Swedish*
Kwek-kwek · *Indonesian*
Vach-vach · *Turkish*
Wack-wack · *Swiss German*
Rap-rap · *Danish*
Gua-gua · *Japanese*
Ga-ga · *Chinese*
Garb-garb · *Thai*

How does a bird sing?

Tweet-tweet · *English*

Kwee-kwee · *French*

Jack-jack · *Korean*

Ji-ji · *Chinese*

Ti-vi-li-lie · *German*

Ti-ti-tyy · *Finnish*

Pi-pi-pi · *Swiss German*

Tsioo-tsioo · *Greek*

Trit-trit · *Indonesian*

Jip-jip · *Thai*

Chic-chiric · *Russian*

Qa-qa · *Ethiopian*

Jikk-jikk · *Turkish*

Czwir-czwir · *Polish*

Chir-chir · *Lithuanian*

Peechiko-pachiko · *Japanese*

So when animals talk,
It can get confusing.
But listen to them,
Not just the humans.

Then make up your own sounds,
There's no need for anguish.
You've just learned the limits
Of all human language.